ONE GOD, ONE WORLD

The Bible and Our Expanding Faith

by

CLARENCE TUCKER CRAIG

Professor of New Testament Language and Literature,
Oberlin Graduate School of Theology

ASSOCIATION PRESS
New York: 347 Madison Avenue

FLEMING H. REVELL COMPANY
New York: 158 Fifth Avenue
1943

The Pioneering Church Series

To THE PEOPLES of all lands, the oneness of the world is now a reality. But in the face of expanding geographical horizons, they are suffering from the lack of comparable spiritual horizons. The keener spirits are asking for a source of perspective that will put the world together and enable them to look at its problems whole. They are seeking a dynamic adequate to our day, rooted in truths that are universal and concerned for humanity everywhere.

It is most important for us to know that there is not only one world but one God, who is creator and ruler of that world, and that he is to be found and understood supremely in the character of the one from whom our religion takes its name. The proper reading of the Bible will reveal the reality of God. It will disclose the significance of the concern of Jesus for a total world enterprise in every generation, but particularly in a time like ours.

This little book by Dr. Craig, *One God, One World—The Bible and Our Expanding Faith,* is intended as such an interpretation of the Biblical sources of our universal faith. This study is one in a series of succinct and timely treatments, called into being through the initiative of representative Christian leaders, to deal with the subject of the pioneering Church.

The books constitute a united approach to the pioneering role of the Christian world community, both in its geographical extension and in the responsibility of its individual members toward areas of unmet need in every phase of human life. It is hoped that this series will fill a useful place in developing both a world-wide Christian view and a new depth of concern for the world Christian task.

ALSO PUBLISHED

God and the Day's Work, by Robert L. Calhoun

To Glorify God, by E. Fay Campbell, James H. Nichols, and James P. Alter

Preface

THE AMERICAN PEOPLE are discovering the world as they have never done before. When the Foreign Policy Association published a description of the parts of the world where our fighting forces were located at that time, it included thirty-two different islands and countries. If the United States ever did believe that it could remain isolated from the rest of the world, that illusion has been completely dissipated. On a planet as small as this, we are all bound together in one bundle of life. No nation can find freedom, security, or prosperity by itself; today it is "all or none." No wonder an organization has been established to promote "world citizenship."

There is nothing new in this for men and women of Christian faith. Its messengers are to be found in practically every country on the globe. Thousands of them have gone out from our own country. When Wendell Willkie returned from his flight around the world, he named these missionaries first in his list of the advance guard of good will toward America. It is an inherent part of Christian faith that God is the father of all men. We cannot worship him and at the same time cut ourselves off from any of his children or deny responsibility toward them. The Christian does not need to join an organization promoting world citizenship; he already belongs to a truly world society, the Church of the living God.

But not all who bear the name of "Christian" realize these truths. One way to enter into their fuller appreciation is to study the crisis that has developed in the modern world through the absence of effective world organization and an adequate spiritual basis for modern civilization. Another is to study the historical ground for the world implications of the gospel as we find it in the Bible. The aim of this booklet is to follow this second approach, to set forth in a brief series of studies the universal aspects of the Christian message.

An open-minded study of the Bible reveals many levels of religious experience and widely differing conceptions. A literature extending over more than a thousand years and written by scores of writers is naturally of unequal value. We shall find a story of developing insights into the nature of God and his expectations for men. We cannot interpret this literature simply in terms of evolution from the lower to the higher. There is no law of progress in spiritual inspiration. While the primitive is usually early, decadence is to be found later as well as progress. In apprehension of religious truth, in contrast to material development and mechanical invention, there is no reason to expect that the best is still ahead of us. It is the Christian faith that revealing acts of God have already taken place. The record of these is truly termed the "word of God." To its pages we turn to gain a fresh glimpse for ourselves of the universal implications of our faith.

Throughout this work, the Biblical quotations are from *The Complete Bible: An American Translation,* by J. M. Powis Smith and Edgar J. Goodspeed. These are used by arrangement with the University of Chicago Press, Chicago.

Contents

CHAPTER I

The Attainment of Monotheism

Real atheists and genuine monotheists are compara-
tively few. Most people believe in a god, for your god
is what you believe in. Yet relatively few believe that there
is only *one* God. There are even some Christians who are
really tritheists rather than trinitarians, for they worship
three different deities: God the Father, Christ, and the
Holy Ghost. Others believe in God and the Devil, or God
and chance, or God and fate, or God and country. The old
pagan deities did not perish even in so-called Christian
countries; the worshipers of Mars, Venus, and Bacchus are
still with us.

Spiritual unity is never possible on a polytheistic basis.
As long as I worship my God and you worship yours, we
are inevitably divided. A polytheistic world is a world of
clashing loyalties. This is a division of which many of us
have personal experience, for our own allegiance is divided
among various gods. We have not yet integrated our experience into a *universe*, but pursue competing ideals. Yet
discovery, invention, and science have brought humanity
together. Distance has been annihilated, and people no
longer pursue their divisive worship in a corner. Can our
world find a basis for spiritual unity?

There are various roads to monotheism. One lies through
intellectual speculation. Pure thought has led men to as-

cribe a unitary origin to the world and to find a single principle upholding it. God is one. In other words, all the gods that men worship are essentially one. This road to monotheism irons out the differences by leading them back to one ultimate principle. It was the approach of much Greek philosophy, impelled by the passion for unity of thought. It has also been the approach of Hindu philosophy, with its elaborate speculations on the one behind the many. Yet, on this basis, the *worship* of many gods persists. It is no accident that the religion of Greece remained polytheistic and that there are many gods in the pantheon of Hinduism. Although thinkers conceive of God as one, under whatever name he may be approached, the contrasting ideals remain.

The other approach to monotheism has been through the assertion that there is only one God. In their ignorance, men may worship various deities; but only one of them is really God. Sometimes the universal sway of *our* God has justified the unlimited extension of the sway of his people. This type of imperialism is illustrated in ancient Babylonia and Egypt, where Marduk and Amun were hailed as the *only God* because their respective worshipers sought universal conquest. Types of this kind of political monotheism are to be found in modern Japan and Germany. It is always a peril lurking in monotheistic faith. We shall see that Israel did not always keep free from the conception that since the Lord alone was God, Jerusalem must become the capital of the entire world (Isaiah 49:22). In the long history of Christian missions, it must be confessed that they have sometimes been used as the advance guard for political penetration. A spiritual imperialism may be as corrosive and arrogant as an economic imperialism.

The development of Biblical monotheism, however, fol-

2

lowed an entirely different pattern. It did not arise through intellectual speculation or a craving for a unitary explanation of the world; nor did it accompany imperialistic expansion, for Israel was always a very tiny nation. Strangely, monotheism came to its most conscious expression during a period of military defeat and political subjugation. Men were led to the sublime heights of monotheistic faith through their appreciation of the universality of moral principles. Justice that is really justice knows no boundaries; true righteousness overleaps every national frontier. Israel was led to an *ethical monotheism*.

Since our purpose does not include a detailed study of the history of Jewish religion, we do not need to raise the moot question of what the worship of Yahweh (the name for Israel's God) meant to Moses. The practical question was that he alone should be worshiped by the people of Israel. The relation between this God and these desert tribes was not a natural relation, but one that was based on a free covenant which this God had made with them. It demanded that this people should be completely loyal to him. He was a "jealous" God who commanded, "You shall have no other gods before me." When the danger of apostasy to the Tyrian Baal was great, Elijah insisted that they must choose between Baal or the Lord; there was no possibility of combining the two.

Many primitive ideas of deity are to be found in the earlier portions of the Old Testament. In the Song of Deborah, it seems to be thought that the Lord comes from the distant mountain of Sinai (Judges 5:4). When Jacob dreamed of a ladder reaching up into the sky, that appeared to him to be the home of the Lord (Genesis 28:12). David seemed to feel that when he was driven out of Palestine,

3

he was outside of the Lord's special sphere (I Samuel 26:19). When the Israelites exchanged their nomadic life for agricultural pursuits in Palestine, it took them a long time to realize that the God who had led them in their desert wanderings also gave the harvest and the vintage. Hosea and the other prophets had to make constant attack on the worship of the agricultural deities of Canaan. It was difficult for men to realize that one God exercised his dominion everywhere and presided over every function of life.

Among primitive peoples, religion affects every interest in life. It is not a special area set apart, but every act concerns a man's religion. Since wars have occupied a large place in man's activity, their gods have inevitably gone with them to war. Israel was no exception, and Yahweh was a God of war who led them in battle (Isaiah 42:13). A natural conclusion from a nation's defeat in battle is that their god has met with a stronger. What more logical course of action, therefore, than to accept the gods of the conquering people! But, thanks to her great prophets, Israel never drew that conclusion. The northern kingdom was overthrown by Assyria in 721 B.C., and many of her people were carried into captivity. The southern kingdom of Judah fell before the conquering armies of Babylonia a little over a century later. In fact, except for a relatively brief period, the Hebrew people were always tributary to the world empire of the moment. Yet the prophets insisted that Israel's disasters were due, not to the feebleness of her God, but to her own sinfulness.

Amos was the earliest of these great creative spokesmen for God. He insisted that the Lord presided over the destinies of all nations (Amos 9:7):

4

> "Are you not like the Ethiopians in my sight,
>   O Israelites?"; it is an oracle of the Lord.
> "Did I not bring up Isreal from the land of Egypt,
>   Also the Philistines from Caphtor, and the Syrians
>   from Kir?"

It was true that there was a special relation of Israel to the Lord, but greater opportunity only meant greater responsibility (Amos 3:2) :

> You only have I known,
> Of all the families of the earth.
> Therefore, will I punish you
> For all your wrong-doing.

In stinging words, he predicted doom for his nation because of their social wrongs (Amos 2:6–7a) :

> For three transgressions of Israel,
> And for four, I will not turn it back;
> Because they have sold the innocent for silver,
> And the needy for the sake of a pair of sandals.
> And they trample upon the heads of the poor,
> And they turn the humble from the way.

The Lord was not pleased with their elaborate ritual, for he was an ethical God. "Let justice roll down like waters, and righteousness like a perennial stream" (Amos 5:24).

Assyria was the world power of the time; her conquering armies were soon to appear. But the prophets proclaimed that doom came, not from a heathen empire, but from their own God of righteousness. Years earlier, Nathan had not hesitated to rebuke King David for conspiring to take the wife of one of his generals (I Kings 11–12), and Elijah had threatened King Ahab for contriving the murder of Naboth because he would not sell his vineyard (I Kings 21). If the king did not stand above the claims of justice, certainly his people did not. The Lord was bringing punishment upon Israel for their sins, and his instrument was the most cruel and barbarous power of the time. The barbarians have always been the executors of divine judgment upon the self-satisfied civilizations of the world.

Isaiah proclaimed the prophetic message in stern words of condemnation (Isaiah 10:5–6):

> Oh! Assyria, rod of my anger, and staff of my fury!
> Against a godless nation I send him,
> And against the people of my wrath I charge him,
> To spoil them, and to prey on them,
> And to trample them down like mire of the streets.

A century later, when Babylonia was the claimant to world dominion, Jeremiah faced the same problem and met it with the same answer. A God of righteousness must visit Israel with punishment for her sins (Jeremiah 4:7–8 and 13:22–25):

> A lion has gone up from his thicket,
> A destroyer of nations—
> He has broken loose from his place,
> To make your land a desolation,
> That your cities may be ravaged,
> And left without inhabitant.
> Gird on sackcloth for this,
> Lament, and wail;
> For the glowing anger of the Lord
> Has not turned back from us.

And if you say to yourself,
"Why have these things befallen me?"
It is for your many sins that your skirts are stripped off,
That your person is outraged.
Can the Ethiopian change his skin,

        Or the leopard his spots?
Then may you also do good,
        Who are trained to do evil.
I will scatter you like drifting stubble
        Before the wind of the desert.
This is your lot, your portion assigned by me,
        Is the oracle of the Lord.

It was after these crushing humiliations had come to
Israel and Judah that the clearest expression was given to
the truth that the Lord alone was God. An unknown
prophet from the time of the exile, whose writings have
been collected in the later chapters of the Book of Isaiah,
proclaimed it over and over again. Here the message is that
of salvation rather than doom, for the disastrous blow had
already fallen. A dispersed and defeated people must rise
again to exalt the Lord who alone is God. As the spokesman
of the Lord he writes (Isaiah 43:10-11 and 45:5-6):

> Before me was no God formed,
> And after me there shall be none:
> I, I, am the Lord,
> And apart from me there is no savior.
>
> I am the Lord, and there is no other—
> Except me there is no God.
> I will gird you, though you knew me not,
> That men may know, from the east
> And from the west, that apart from me there is none.

This full ethical monotheism had three important implications. If one God was the ultimate fact, he must be *the
creator of the universe*. The prophet of the exile repeatedly
affirmed this (Isaiah 40:28 and 45:12):

> The Lord is a God everlasting,
> The Creator of the ends of the earth.

7

> I made the earth,
> And created man upon it;
> My hand stretched out the heavens,
> And all their host I marshalled;

Here is a world view that does not identify God and the world, as in the mystic pantheisms, which lead logically to the worship of the powers of nature. The God of the Bible is one who transcends the world yet does not dwell apart from it in splendid isolation. He has expressed something of his will through his creation, but the creature is never to be confused with the creator. God is not simply the sum of the natural powers that we behold; he is the artist who has revealed himself in a limited way through the works of his hand.

A second implication of monotheistic faith is *the absurdity of all forms of idolatry.* The supreme God of all the earth cannot be pictured in any image fashioned by men. Surrounded as they were by many forms of idolatrous worship, the Jews presented a striking contrast in their insistence upon the spiritual nature of the Lord. The prophet described the making of idols with withering scorn (Isaiah 40:18-19 and 41:6-7):

> To whom, then, would you liken God,
> Or what likeness would you place over against him?
> An idol! the smelter casts it,
> And the goldsmith overlays it with gold,
> And fastens it with silver links.
> Each one helps his fellow,
> And says to his comrade, "Have courage!"
> The smelter cheers on the goldsmith,
> He that smooths with the hammer him that strikes
>   with the mallet,
> Saying of the rivetting, "It is good!"
> As he fastens it with nails so that it cannot move.

The modern danger is not that we shall bow down before graven images. We know that artistic material symbols may give wings to the spirit, enkindle our imagination, and suggest to the mind what can never be pictured; but we are never tempted to believe that these are gods. The form of idolatry of which we are more in danger is the identification of the mental images of God that we create with God himself. Although our conceptions of God are always inadequate, that is no reason to reject our belief in God. No human idol, whether it be material object or mental image, is God himself.

The third implication of monotheism is that *God may be worshiped anywhere*. A truly universal God may be approached in any place where the contrite heart sincerely seeks him. It is true that the idea arose among some who were zealous for the temple at Jerusalem that if there was only one God, there was also only one place to worship. The condition of exile, which removed many devout from the center of worship, made that question acute. Jeremiah had the truer insight when he wrote to the exiles (Jeremiah 29:12–13):

You shall call me, and I will answer you; you shall pray to me, and I will listen to you; you shall seek me, and you shall find me; for when you seek me with all your heart, I will let myself be found by you, is the oracle of the Lord.

Here is the conception of a God whom no missionary needs to take to India, China, or the isles of the sea; for he has always been there. Men need only to learn how to turn to him.

But it is never easy for anyone to hold to this ethical monotheism. Life is far from simple, and there is much in experience that seems to contradict the idea that a God of justice and love is the ultimate determiner of destiny and the arbiter of world history. The author of the Book of Job reflected on many of these problems; he did not reach a theoretical solution, but still he clung to his faith. Many of the deeper spirits of the later Judaism came to recognize the presence of many God-opposing spiritual forces. But they never accepted an ultimate dualism. The God who had made all things good would, in the end, restore the perfection of his creation. There were not two ultimate principles but one; "And the Lord shall become king over all the earth" (Zechariah 14:9).

CHAPTER II

The Servant of the Lord

THE ETHICAL MONOTHEISM that arose in ancient Judaism was a unique spiritual development. Nowhere else was there such a belief in a living God of justice and mercy who spoke to the prophet who was attuned to hear his word, and who acted in history for judgment and salvation. When we refer to this as God's revelation, it is because *persons* are only known as they reveal themselves. *Things* are discovered; *persons* must make themselves known if their true nature is ever to become apparent. For the Jews, God was not a vague impersonal essence; he was the living God who entered into personal relations with his people.

We should not think of Israel, however, as living entirely apart from the rest of the world while she cherished this noble treasure. She was in constant contact with other peoples and inevitably absorbed much from the environment about her. Religion cannot remain static, any more than any other aspect of life. Everything that is alive must grow and change. Only what is inert and dead remains unchanged. But there are always two directions in which change may take place. It may mean enlargement and growth of that which is the distinctive essence, or it may mean change into something different through the absorption of alien elements. How did the faith of ancient Israel react to its environment?

Much of her sacrificial system had Canaanitic roots, but the prophetic religion of Israel never gave approval to such immoral rites as sacred prostitution. Many current myths were absorbed, but when the Hebrew storytellers told of a flood destroying mankind, it had an ethical purpose. In each version of the creation story, every polytheistic element was eliminated. The prophets were continually fighting against the paganizing of the worship of the Lord. It was in order to preserve its purity that this was confined to the one shrine at Jerusalem, symbolic of his unity. Yet it was always a difficult struggle. Ezekiel reveals that pagan practices of sun worship intruded even into the temple (although this element did not contaminate the central line of religious development).

With the loss of their separate political existence, the Jews were more and more in danger of their being absorbed into the surrounding peoples and their religion being merged with other cults. The Israelites exiled at the fall of Samaria were apparently "lost" in this way. In considering the narrowness of the later Judaism, we must never forget this peril that they were combatting. The ethical monotheism of the Jews might never have been preserved if their leaders had not been so intent upon resisting foreign spiritual influences. The "broad-minded" Jews, for whom all religions were more or less the same, were not the ones who preserved their unique heritage. Willingness to be different in the face of contemptuous ridicule was the price that many noble spirits had to pay in order to keep the worship of the living God from being swallowed up in a sea of paganism.

Nehemiah built a wall about the city of Jerusalem (Nehemiah 2:1-6, 15); that was for the protection of the holy city. But Ezra and the priests and scribes who followed him built an even higher wall about the Jewish people. The preservation of their distinctive national customs was made a solemn religious duty. All intermarriage with foreigners was strictly forbidden, for foreign wives would bring with them alien religious conceptions (Nehemiah 13:23–27). Naturally, many Jews protested against this. The little Book of Ruth came from the pen of one with more tolerant impulses. His apparently innocent pastoral idyll told the story of the marriage of Ruth, a Moabitess, to Boaz, an ancestor of David. In other words, if this legislation had been in force at that time, Israel would never have had her most glorious king. Nevertheless, the ideal of racial exclusiveness continued.

Yet, with all their stubborn resistance to foreign influences, the Jews were not unaffected in their religion by the cultural environments in which they lived. It is not difficult for Old Testament scholars to locate the portions of the Old Testament that were written in the "Greek" period. One of the clearest cases of change in religious point of view lay in the adoption by most Jews of the idea of the resurrection of the dead (Daniel 12:1–2). This meant that the Lord would not only vindicate the nation "in the latter days," by establishing his rule through them, but would also raise up the righteous individuals of all time to participate in that rule. This change from the earlier belief was almost certainly adopted under Persian religious influences. Still, it may rightly be claimed that it was a development of the *genius* of Jewish faith, rather than a compromise with competing ideals. It was a logical extension of their faith to the life of the individual.

Although the essential purity of the ethical monotheistic

faith was maintained, nevertheless there remained an inner contradiction. The Jews believed that the Lord was the only God, and that he was a God of righteousness. How, then, could he be the God of but one people? If his sway was universal, must not his worship be just as world-wide? If the one God had revealed his true nature to Israel, how could they leave the rest of the world in the darkness of their ignorant worship? Did not a national religion mean a denial of essential monotheism?

Amos had taught that privilege brought *accountability* before God. The great prophet of the exile added the truth of *responsibility* to make him known to all men. Israel was the servant of the Lord; she had been scattered abroad in order to bring knowledge of him to all peoples. Their monotheism was not to be a selfish privilege, but it laid obligations upon them. The Lord speaks to Israel through the voice of the prophet (Isaiah 42:6 and 49:6):

> I the Lord have called you of set purpose,
> And have grasped you by the hand;
> I have kept you, and have made you a pledge to the
>   people,
>   A light to the nations.
>
> It is too slight a thing for your being my servant
> That I should but raise up the tribes of Jacob
> And restore the survivors of Israel;
> So I will make you a light of the nations,
> That my salvation may reach to the end of the earth.

And to the nations, he proclaims this word (Isaiah 51:4 and 45:22, 24):

> Hearken to me, O peoples,
> O nations, give ear to me!
> For instruction shall go forth from me,
> And my truth as a light to the peoples.

> Turn to me, and be saved,
>> All ends of the earth!

> That to me every knee shall bow,
>> Every tongue shall swear,
> Saying, "Only in the Lord
>> Is victory and strength."

Sometimes the servant of the Lord is presented by the prophet as a suffering servant. It has long been debated whether this figure stood for the loyal remnant in Israel or for one of her great leaders (possibly Jeremiah or Zerubbabel), or whether it referred to some individual yet to arise. In any case, the passages give a majestic portrayal of that vicarious suffering which brings redemption to others. The longest and the greatest of the poems should be read entire and in its context to get the sweep of the prophet's conception, for so many individual verses have become associated in our minds with their application to Jesus (52:13–53:12).

The prophet represents the nations as speaking about this despised servant, of whom they now come to realize that (Isaiah 53:5):

> He was pierced for our transgressions,
> He was crushed for our iniquities;
> The chastisement of our welfare was upon him,
> And through his stripes we were healed.

At the close of the chapter, the prophet gives the Lord's interpretation of this figure (Isaiah 53:11):

> Through his affliction shall my servant, the Righteous One
>> bring righteousness to many,
> And shall carry the burden of their guilt.

Here, monotheistic faith is not looked upon as the exclusive privilege of the Jews, but as a treasure of which they are the trustee, one that they must carry to all the nations even at the price of suffering and humiliation.

It must be confessed that there are relatively few expressions of this point of view in the Old Testament. The greatest missionary book is the little tract that tells the story of the prophet Jonah. It portrays one of the great miracles of all time, but it will never be discovered by readers who ponder over the possibility of a man's living three days in the belly of a whale. Jonah was typical of the ancient Jew who did not believe in foreign missions and who had no desire to shed any light for the benefit of the despised Gentiles. When the word of the Lord came to him that he should preach in Nineveh, capital of the hated Assyrian kingdom, he tried to run away from this call to become a foreign missionary by taking a ship bound for Tarshish. But the Lord would not let him escape his duty and sent a storm on the sea. Even when Jonah allowed himself to be thrown overboard to appease the angry deity, the Lord did not let him get away, but provided a means to restore him to dry land.

When the call came to Jonah a second time, he knew that it was useless to run away. He still had no love or compassion for the people of Assyria, and he went primarily to witness the destruction of the hated city. But instead of being heedless to the prophet's message, its inhabitants repented in sackcloth and ashes. Poor Jonah sat down outside the city in bitter disappointment. Then, through the parable of a gourd, the Lord showed him that the divine mercy and love extended even to their national enemies (Jonah 4:6) :

You have had pity on the gourd, for which you did not toil; nor did you raise it; which grew in a night, and perished in a night! And should not I, indeed, have pity on Nineveh, that great city, wherein are more than a hundred and twenty thousand infants that cannot distinguish between their right hand and their left, and much cattle?

Many Jews did carry on missionary activity and win others to their faith. Our information concerning the lands to the east is too meager to draw reliable conclusions, but scholars are able to estimate that the Jews comprised 7 per cent of the population of the Roman Empire in the first century. They were scattered far and wide. It would seem clear that these numbers were not simply the result of natural propagation, but that many Gentiles had been won to their faith. Besides the full proselytes who were received, each synagogue became a center for "God-fearers"—men and women drawn by the pure monotheism and lofty ethic of the Jews, but who were not willing to become incorporated into the Jewish nation. For even among the most broad-minded Jews, this contradiction remained. The Lord alone was God, but in order to worship him it was necessary to become a part of this one nation and to obey its peculiar mores.

The Jewish people did not accept their status of a small tributary nation as final. They looked forward to the time, "in the latter days," when the Lord would exalt them and make Jerusalem the center of his rule. For some, that was to be a time of vengeance upon their oppressors; but others stressed the Lord's universal sway over all peoples (Isaiah 2:2-3):

> Now in the end of the days
> The mountain of the Lord's house will be
> Established on the top of the mountains,
>   And lifted above the hills.

17

And all the nations will stream to it,
Many peoples will go and say:
"Come! let us go up to the mountain of the Lord,
To the house of the God of Jacob;
That he may instruct us in his ways,
And that we may walk in his paths;
For out of Zion goes forth instruction,
The word of the Lord out of Jerusalem."

In many of the Jewish writings coming from near the time of Jesus, this wider outlook is to be found. Among these is the Book of Enoch, which is quoted in the letter of Jude and in which may be found many of the terms and ideas in our gospels. There we read, "All nations shall offer me adoration and praise, and all will worship me (Enoch 10:21). It is the one pre-Christian book where the term "Son of man" is used as it is in the gospels (Enoch 48:4):

(That Son of man) will be a staff to the righteous on which they will support themselves and not fall, and he will be the light of the Gentiles and the hope of those who are troubled of heart.

Yet, even in these passages, the hope for the future is expressed in terms of a spiritual imperialism. The rule of God is not distinguished from the rule of the one nation that had received the revelation of his true nature. When the nations of the world accept the sovereignty of the Lord, they must also accept the peculiar customs of this one people. The law of God includes not only justice, honesty, truthfulness, and love, but dietary regulations, non-moral taboos, and customs that had been hallowed by the history of this one people. The dominant ideals of rule were the pagan ideals of might and force. Only with difficulty did they keep the proud arrogance of a "superior nation" from

18

corroding their relations with others, even when they held true to the ideal of being a "light to the Gentiles." In other words, a *religious* nationalism simply could not be united with a true universalism. If the Lord alone was God, it should not mean that all men must become Jews. That was inherently inconsistent with the ethical character ascribed to God. Another way must be found, and that way led through the figure of Jesus of Nazareth.

CHAPTER III

Jesus and the Kingdom of God

JESUS is the central figure of Christian faith. In him, God's purpose found its consummation. Nevertheless, he cannot be divorced from his Jewish heritage. He lived and died a Jew. The ideals and hopes of his people provided the background for his teaching and his life career. Still, he was such a revolutionary prophet that his own people rejected him. The movement to which he gave birth could not be kept within their narrow religious fold, but was soon to burst its dikes and ultimately cover the world.

The deep roots of Jesus in his ancestral faith are made clear by his central message. The earliest gospel summarized it in the words, "The time has come and the reign of God is near; repent, and believe this good news" (Mark 1:15). Although the exact phrase, "the reign of God," is not to be found in the Old Testament, the idea had had a long history among the Jews. God as creator was king in the world that he had made. That sovereignty, however, had been broken by human sin. Now the reign of God was confined to those loyal individuals who, by obedience to his law, took upon themselves "the yoke of the kingdom." But, as we have seen, they looked forward to the day when God would intervene and re-establish his rule. Sometimes this involved the political subjugation of the nations; sometimes it was thought of in terms of a reconstituted earth. But the continuing thread in all of their varied ideas was the coming of the perfect rule of God among men.

Jesus never defined the kingdom of God. That was unnecessary, for everyone knew what was meant. He proclaimed the good news that it was near, so near in fact that its powers were already present in his own ministry. The sick were being healed, and the poor receiving good news. This was the first new note struck by Jesus: the reign of God was so near that the glow of its light was already shining upon them.

A second original emphasis lay in the description of those who would enter God's kingdom (Luke 6:20-21) :

> Blessed are you who are poor, for the Kingdom of God is yours!
> Blessed are you who are hungry now, for you will be satisfied!
> Blessed are you who weep now, for you will laugh!

In other words, the reign of God was not for the rich who benefited from the injustices of the present age. Riches were not a sign of God's favor. "It is easier for a camel to get through the eye of a needle than for a rich man to get into the Kingdom of God" (Mark 10:25).

There were other radically new emphases in the description of those who would enter God's reign. Contemporary religion exalted the wise scribe who was deeply versed in the minutiae of the law. But Jesus took a little child and placed him in the midst, saying, "Whoever does not accept the Kingdom of God like a child shall not enter it at all" (Mark 10:15). The supremely religious group in Palestine was the Pharisees. In their zeal to apply God's law to all of life, they formed associations of the pious to avoid all contaminating contacts. But Jesus was sure that this led to self-righteousness, rather than to true goodness. Entrance to the kingdom of God lay only through the narrow door of repentance, and it was those who prided themselves on their piety who found that most difficult. Hence he said to them, "The tax-gatherers and prostitutes are going into the Kingdom of God ahead of you" (Matthew 21:31).

One of the most striking aspects of Jesus' description of those who would enter the kingdom of God is the absence of anything that emphasized Jewish peculiarities. Jesus did not reject the ritual requirements of the law, but his carelessness toward them was a constant source of criticism from strict Pharisees. He did not bless those who were pure according to Jewish ritual requirements; it was the "pure in heart" who would see God in his kingdom. A Gentile could be an example of faith, and a Samaritan of love toward neighbors. The model of perfection was not Abraham or Moses or any other Jewish hero; it was God, the father of all men.

Much of the teaching of Jesus about the kingdom of God was cast into parables. He dealt, not in abstract definitions, but in vivid comparisons with the everyday experiences of life. Various aspects of the rule of God and of man's relation to that rule were described by means of stories that the simplest and unlearned could understand. Unfortunately, they are not always so easy for us to understand, since we read many of them apart from their original context and are hampered by a long tradition of allegorizing in the Christian Church. It should be remembered that a parable is an expanded simile and that, like a simile, it has one point of comparison. In an allegory, on the other hand, many features have separate meanings that need interpretation.

As we turn to some typical parables of Jesus, we must seek to find the one point of comparison between this story out of life and the kingdom of God. One of the most striking is preserved only in Mark (Mark 4:26–29):

The reign of God is like a man scattering seed on the ground, and then sleeping at night and getting up by day, while the seed sprouts and comes up, without his knowing it. The ground of itself is productive, putting forth first a blade, then a head, then fully developed wheat in the head. But as soon as the crop will let him, the man goes in with his sickle, for the harvest time has come.

In what way is the kingdom of God like this familiar experience in the life of a farmer? Obviously, the point of comparison does not lie in a long, gradual period of growth, for wheat ripens in a few months. Rather, just as the crop depends ultimately on forces outside of man's control, so is it with the kingdom of God. Even while man sleeps, the rain, the sunshine, and the soil bring forth the harvest. So God must *send* his reign, and for its coming man is to *pray*, "Thy kingdom come." This same idea recurs in other comparisons used by Jesus. "The Kingdom of Heaven is like yeast, which a woman took and buried in a bushel of flour until it had all risen" (Matthew 13:33). Here again is expressed the certainty of a complete transformation by powers that are independent of man. *Man does not labor to carve a better world out of a neutral universe, but God himself is the surety for his coming reign.*

We have seen how Jesus extended the invitation to the kingdom of God to all and how he ignored the exclusive assumptions of the Pharisees. This aspect of unmerited mercy in God's rule was expressed in many stories. Among the most striking is the story of a feast, for the new age had

23

often been compared to a banquet (Matthew 22:2–5, 8–10):

The Kingdom of Heaven is like a king, who gave a wedding banquet for his son. And he sent his slaves to summon those who had been invited to the banquet, and they would not come. He sent other slaves a second time, and said to them, "Tell those who have been asked, 'Here I have my banquet all ready, my bullocks and fat cattle are killed, and everything is ready. Come to the banquet!' " But they took no notice of it, and went off, one to his estate, another to his business.

Then the king said to his slaves, "The banquet is ready, but those who were invited have proved unworthy of it. So go out where the roads leave the city and invite everyone you find to the banquet." So his slaves went out on the roads, and got together all the people they could find, good or bad, and the hall was filled with guests.

In other words, just as a human host wants his banquet table filled with guests, so God now extends the invitation to all. Since the religious leaders of the Jews were not repenting at the summons, the invitation must be extended to others.

Everyone is familiar with the parable of the prodigal son, and the stories of the lost sheep and the lost coin (Luke 15). They were told to emphasize the seeking love of God and his joy at the recovery of the lost. All of these stories make clear that entrance into the kingdom of God is not something a man earns by the merit of his punctilious observance of the ritual law; but, in the last analysis, it is a *gift of God's love*. The religious word for this is "grace," goodness that man does not deserve. Over and over again, Jesus emphasized that the kingdom was not a reward to be earned but a gift to be received. The kingdom of Heaven is like an employer who pays the same wages to those who have worked one hour as to those who have labored all day (Matthew 20:1-15). In other words, it is not a wage at all, but a gift. A slave cannot earn a reward from his master, for after he has done all he still owes service. So, in man's relation to God, after he has done all he is still an unrighteous servant, and whatever he receives must be a gift of grace (Luke 17:7-10).

At the same time, Jesus taught that the coming of the kingdom of God meant *judgment*. It brought woes on the unrepentant as well as beatitudes for the humble-minded and merciful. Matthew appended to the parable quoted above the incident of a wedding guest upon whom the most severe judgment fell. Jesus did not think in terms of the gradual transformation of society into a perfect world, but he expected a crisis that would bring doom for many. "The road that leads to destruction is broad and spacious, and there are many who go in by it" (Matthew 7:13). Heathen cities like Tyre and Sidon would fare better in the coming judgment than Chorazin, Bethsaida, and Capernaum, which had turned a deaf ear to his call for repentance. If they did not repent, they would perish like the Galileans, whose blood Pilate mingled with the sacrifices. Jesus pictured the threatening doom in the figure of an unfruitful fig tree (Luke 13:6-9):

A man had a fig tree growing in his garden, and he went to look for fruit on it, and could not find any. And he said to the gardener, "Here I have come three years to look for fruit on this fig tree, without finding any. Cut it down. Why should it waste the ground?" He answered, "Let it stand this one year more sir, till I dig around it and manure it; perhaps it will bear fruit next year. But if it does not, you can have it cut down."

Nowhere in the gospels does Jesus speak of "building"

the kingdom of God. That is a quite un-Biblical idea. If the reign of God is to come, God must act in judgment on man's sin and bestow his gracious gift. Some Americans are afraid to accept this truth for fear that it will lead to an unwholesome quietism. But certainly the example and precept of Jesus were not such as to encourage anyone simply to sit down and fold his hands as he waited upon God, for his own life was filled with good deeds. When he called men to follow him, he placed the highest evaluation on feeding the hungry, clothing the naked, healing the sick, and showing mercy to those in need. So, although men do not build a kingdom of God, they have very vital tasks to perform.

First of all, men are called upon *to repent*. No one can repent for another, not even God; and the "righteous" who imagine that they have no need of repentance only shut themselves out of the realm of God. In Chapter IV, we shall examine more closely the radical exposition of the will of God that Jesus gave. He did not rest content in compromises with the present sinful age, but faced men with the absolute standards of God. To repent is not to be sorry that things have turned out badly. It means more than to try a little harder to do what is right; it means a resolute turning to God, a sorrow for wrongdoing that leads to the reformation of life.

In the second place, men are *to practice deeds of kindness* like those of Jesus. Although he himself never spoke of his founding the kingdom of God, Jesus did refer to the healings that he performed as signs of the presence of the kingdom. "If I am driving the demons out by the aid of God's Spirit then the Kingdom of God has overtaken you" (Matthew 12:28). When his disciples were sent out, they too were to heal the sick. Even the giving of a cup of cold water had its value as an expression of the spirit of Christ. "It is not everyone who says to me, 'Lord, Lord!' who will get into the Kingdom of Heaven, but only those who do the will of my Father in heaven" (Matthew 7:21).

Again, Jesus laid the emphasis on the need for *the forgiving spirit* if men were to enter God's kingdom. Man could never enter on the basis of his own goodness, but only through the forgiving mercy of God. There was only one condition for receiving that forgiveness, a willingness to forgive those who wrong us. That was stated clearly in the Lord's Prayer, "Forgive us our debts, as we have forgiven our debtors" (Matthew 6:12). It was especially emphasized in one of the hyperbolic parables. Matthew's version begins with the words, "The Kingdom of Heaven may be compared with a king who resolved to settle accounts with his slaves" (Matthew 18:23 ff.). It is a parable of the kingdom, because the forgiving attitude toward others is necessary if man is to enter. The slave who owed ten million dollars had his debt canceled because he asked for it. When he went out and demanded payment from a fellow-slave who owed him twenty dollars, the direct punishment fell on him. Similarly, our debt to God is an unpayable obligation. Man cannot ask for its forgiveness, if he continues to cherish an unforgiving attitude toward his brother.

Finally, man must *strive with all his might to enter the kingdom of God*. It is the supreme good in life that is worth any price it may cost (Matthew 13:44-46):

The Kingdom of Heaven is like a hoard of money, buried in a field, which a man found, and buried again. And he was overjoyed, and went and sold everything he had and bought the field.

Again, the Kingdom of Heaven is like a dealer in search of

fine pearls. He found one costly pearl, and went and sold everything he had, and bought it.

In other words, no sacrifice is too great to pay. It would be better to cut off a hand or a foot than to miss the kingdom of God. One must be willing to forsake family, friends, possessions, and everything held dear. "No one of you who does not say goodbye to all he has can be a disciple of mine" (Luke 14:33).

Sometimes the Church has lost sight of the message of the coming kingdom of God. Sometimes it has perverted that message in ways far removed from the hope of Jesus. But whenever men truly face him, they are brought back to the thought of the reign of God. Since he spoke, the two have been indivisible. Jesus and the kingdom were inseparable from the very beginning. Although Jesus did not make public claims for himself, the tradition portrays the conviction that he was the anointed king or Messiah. This is not the place to enter into a discussion of all of the intricate historical questions involved, but the belief expressed this religious certainty: the rule of the determiner of destiny is to be exercised through one who came not to be served but to serve, and to give his life for the freedom of many.

CHAPTER IV

The Sermon on the Mount

THE PRIMARY INTEREST in Jesus on the part of the average person today lies in his ethical teaching. Although one may disregard that teaching as impractical, he cannot help but be impressed with its high ideals. Jesus distilled the best moral standards from the ethical wisdom of his people and put them into matchless words, which his followers cherished most highly. He enunciated these sayings, not with the pedantry of the scribe, but with the authority of a prophet who had original insight into truth.

The most compact and systematic collection of the ethical teaching of Jesus is to be found in Matthew 5 to 7. This is the first of five great compilations of the teachings of the Master in this gospel. The Old Testament law was contained in five books. This evangelist thought of Jesus as a new lawgiver whose divine commands were likewise in five books. Just as Moses had ascended a mountain to receive the law from God, so Jesus ascended a mountain to deliver the new and higher law to his disciples. Therefore, this collection is usually called the Sermon on the Mount, although these teachings were undoubtedly brought together from many utterances of Jesus.

We saw in the last study that the center of Jesus' message was the kingdom of God. It was fitting, therefore, to begin this discourse with a description of the kind of people who would enter that kingdom. But in the interval before that age should come, the disciples still lived in a hostile and heathen world. What should be their attitude? Three little parabolic words were placed next to show the influence that the disciples might have: they should be like a lamp, to shed the light of truth about them; they should be like salt, to pervade the whole with a distinctive flavor of goodness; they should be like a city on a hilltop, an unhideable symbol of the presence of God.

The discourse then turns to the *standard for repentance*. For the Jew, that would naturally be the law. It is made clear that Jesus was not an iconoclast, tearing down the established structure of society. He had not come to destroy the law but to fulfil it. He had come to intensify its moral demands so that their full implications would become clearer. Three of the antitheses that follow illustrate this "liberal" attitude toward the law (Matthew 5:20-21):

You have heard that the men of old were told, "You shall not murder," and "Whoever murders will have to answer to the court." But I tell you that anyone who gets angry with his brother will have to answer to the court.

It is clear that Jesus was not offering amendments to the statute books of Palestine. But although courts of law do not convict on the ground of anger, Jesus wanted to make it clear that the real sin lay in the intention of the heart. In the sight of God, it was the murderous hatred that was evil, not simply the overt act.

The other two illustrations are drawn from the laws against adultery and perjury. Similar formulas are used to emphasize that sin does not lie in an unlawful sexual act. It is to be found in the lust of the heart and the impure desire. It is not enough to avoid false oaths; the evil really lies in the practice of dishonesty that requires a man to go on oath that this time he is telling the truth. The demand of God is for absolute honesty, absolute purity, and absolute good will. His standard of goodness calls, not for actions that conform to the requirements of the law, but for motives that correspond to the perfection of God.

A second group of antitheses illustrates an even more radical principle of Jesus. "For I tell you that unless your uprightness is far superior to that of the scribes and Pharisees, you will never even enter the Kingdom of Heaven" (Matthew 5:20). In these illustrations, the outer law is not deepened to its inner intent, but specific concessions are set aside. The husband had the prerogative of divorcing his wife, provided that he gave her a certificate of divorce. But Jesus recognized as the law of God's creation that man and wife should become one and inseparable. The concession of divorce that Moses gave was only because of the hardness of men's hearts.

Likewise, the law of retaliation was set aside (Matthew 6:38–41):

You have heard that they were told, "An eye for an eye and a tooth for a tooth." But I tell you not to resist injury, but if anyone strikes you on your right cheek, turn the other to him too; and if anyone wants to sue you for your shirt, let him have your coat too. And if anyone forces you to go one mile, go two miles with him.

We should not miss what Jesus was saying by this oriental hyperbole. It is not enough to limit retaliation to the wrong that has been received. That may be the basis of statute law in most organized societies, but it is not the righteousness that God demands. This rejects all thought of retaliation and extends love even toward one's enemies. Heathen show reciprocity by doing good to their friends. Jesus said that his disciples were called to the impartiality of God, whose rain and sunshine bless the upright and the wrongdoers alike.

The sermon then turns to *sincerity in worship*. The chief religious practices followed in the contemporary Judaism were almsgiving, prayer, and fasting. Jesus insisted that these were not good works to advertise a man's piety. Their only value lay in the genuineness of the expression of a contrite heart. The Father, who sees what is secret, will reward sincere devotion. Those who do these things hypocritically, to be seen by men, already have all the reward they will get. Fasting and prayer are not to satisfy outward religious regulations. If they do not express an inward yearning of the spirit, they have no value for either God or man.

The next topic is that of *possessions*. The treasures of that day were hoards of gold, fine carpets, and vessels made of precious metal. The disciples were to gather treasures that were not as easily stolen as these. They were to lay up treasure with God by selling these material things that afforded no preparation for entrance into the kingdom of God. Instead, these things were a supreme obstacle, because they claimed the devotion of the heart. "For wherever your treasure is, your heart will be also" (Matthew 6:21). God and Mammon cannot claim the sole devotion at the same time. How could a man love God with his *whole heart* when it was chained to material possessions!

But there is another side to possessions: *the anxious care that results from their absence*. The life of the kingdom of God calls for trust in God's providential provision. If he cares for the birds and clothes the fields, how much more will he care for men (Matthew 7:31–33)?

So do not worry and say, "What shall we have to eat?" or "What shall we have to drink?" or "What shall we have to wear?" For these are all things the heathen are in pursuit of, and your heavenly Father knows well that you need all this. But you must make his kingdom, and uprightness before him, your greatest care, and you will have all these other things besides.

A final series of demands deal with *tolerance* and *service*. Our judgments upon others are always self-judgments as well. The zealous reformer who is so eager to eliminate the slightest flaw from his neighbor should first look toward his own faults. How can a man see to remove a speck from the eye of his neighbor as long as he has a beam in his own? But this toleration does not mean ignoring the needs and shortcomings of others. In word and in deed, Jesus called for *active good will*. Although the Golden Rule is by no means the height of the teaching of Jesus, it offers a valuable principle of conduct. "You must always treat other people as you would like to have them treat you, for this sums up the Law and the Prophets" (Matthew 7:12).

These sayings are so familiar to us that we are apt to overlook the challenge they present to the accepted standards of our day. Obviously, they stand in complete antithesis to the competition of our business world, to the selfish strife in our social life, and to the coercions of political organization. But the Christian is not alone disturbed by the fact that life does not now follow the pattern of the Sermon on the Mount; he is troubled by the question as to whether it ever can. Can these exalted precepts ever be made practicable, considering the sinful bent of human nature? We may agree that these words picture the ideals of a completed kingdom of God, but what relevance can they have

33

now to men who must adjust their lives to the kingdoms of the world? No wonder so many earnest Christians have felt compelled to retire from the world into idealistic colonies where they might pursue these standards among like-minded men and women!

We must note the difference clearly between the Sermon on the Mount and the ideals of "social action" that have become important for many contemporary American Christians. We would use the power of the State to provide economic security for the disadvantaged, to forbid unjust practices in industry, to eliminate slums and conditions conducive to vice and crime. We believe that Christian love should lead to all such social objectives, but this truth must not blind our eyes to the fact that the orientation of the Sermon on the Mount is almost exclusively individual. Jesus was not raising the question as to how men might eliminate the social evils of Palestine; he laid the emphasis on the *inner motives* of men, which can never be touched by outward coercion. He summoned individuals to live above any law that might be enforced in society. When he called upon men to love their enemies, it was not to provide a technique that would throw off the Roman tyranny in a more clever way than by appeal to arms. He never promised that non-retaliation would attain any particular political results, but he did promise that it would make those who practiced it like God.

When these demands are understood, one of two courses must follow: either they will be dismissed as sublime but impracticable, or they will lead even the best of men to a daily repentance before God. If the divine standard is to be found here, if Jesus is right in calling this the expectation of God, then no man is fully righteous in his sight. Jesus included a petition for forgiveness in his model prayer; man will never know the time when he does not need to make

34

that prayer his own. Here are standards that are not relative to human fallibility; nor are they compromises with the sinful society about us. Like the kingdom of God, they are absolute; hence there is no prospect that they will be transcended twenty centuries hence. The Sermon on the Mount points away from any dependence upon man's own goodness to utter reliance on the forgiving love of God. It does not offer an ethic that can be accepted even though Christian faith is denied. Here are standards that can have meaning only for the one who believes that a God of righteousness and love is the ultimate fact.

Many American students have been slow to realize this truth. In their commendable zeal to make the world a better place in which to live, they have had little time to reflect on the implications of the Sermon on the Mount. But this understanding will show how impossible it is to treat all of the Bible on the same level. The Christian Church has found it much easier to make the Ten Commandments the ethical catechism of the Church than this Sermon. But Matthew 5 to 7 towers as far above the Ten Commandments as Jesus does over every other personality of the Bible. The Christian cannot defend his bigoted intolerance, his participation in war, his race discrimination, his pious conformity to outward standards by any appeal to Bible verses as long as he gives Jesus the highest place. Jesus spoke out of repudiation of some Old Testament teaching and dissatisfaction with much of the devout practice of his time. We cannot look upon all of the Bible as equally the word of God and give him the true pre-eminence.

The Christian should not refuse to examine the criticisms that are often made of the standards of Jesus. Although the individual ought to enter upon marriage as a lifelong obligation, is not divorce sometimes the lesser of two evils? Although non-retaliation may be the ideal for individuals, could society ever be organized on that basis? How is a continuing culture possible if men do not lay up treasures on earth? Is it really true that men can depend on God's care for their food and clothing? No wonder Christians have been tempted to explain away these difficult words, to take refuge in the idea of "Oriental hyperbole," and to refuse to be bound by the "literal" words of the Master. Any discussion is certain to reveal differing points of view on these issues.

It is less important that we come together on theoretical opinions than that we find agreement in practice. His words must be taken seriously by all who call Jesus Lord. Although we may differ on human possibilities under the conditions of historical life, it is clear that the Christian's task is to make these ideals progressively realized. Although he fails to attain absolute purity, he can never be satisfied with any less a standard. Although the hearts of men and women may still be hard, he does not believe that the ideal of marriage has been changed. The goal of a Christian is never to vanquish a foe but always to overcome the enmity that divides. Although treasures must be laid up for a continuing society on earth, they should never provide a substitute for work to the few, but an enrichment of the lives of the many. Since God *has* abundantly supplied us with material resources, it is man's duty to distribute these so that no anxious care shall curse the lives of any of his children. Although none of us has attained moral perfection, at least we shall never settle back into complacent self-satisfaction. For through the Sermon on the Mount, there speaks to us the God of judgment as well as the God of grace.

The Personal Contacts of Jesus

THERE ARE MANY POINTS OF VIEW from which the career of Jesus may be examined. In this little study, we have chosen to consider his contacts with persons. The incidents recorded in the gospels appear to have little concern with large world movements. But Jesus was supremely interested in the welfare of individuals. He seemed to feel that if the lives of a few men and women were really transformed, profound results might follow. His human touch on individual need stands out in the traditions that have been preserved.

It is true that Jesus preached to the multitudes who were drawn by his magnetic personality. In teeming villages and in the wilderness, in synagogue and by the lakeside, he brought his announcement of the kingdom of God and the call to repentance. But this work would not have left a lasting impression if Jesus had not gathered about himself a group of disciples. They were called "to be with him," to receive the intimate impact of his teaching and life, and to assist in the work of his itinerant ministry. They were asked, not simply to repent, but "to follow" him in the most literal sense of the word.

Jesus was not a leader who could offer any financial assurances to a Peter who left his fishing boats or a Levi on closing his toll booth; he was a homeless wanderer. "Foxes have holes, and wild birds have nests, but the Son of man has nowhere to lay his head" (Luke 9:58). Following Jesus has such a metaphorical significance for us that we forget what it meant to the first disciples. They were facing a supreme crisis; all merely personal affairs were forced into the background (Luke 9:59-60):

Jesus said to another, "Follow me."
But he said, "Let me first go and bury my father."
Jesus said to him, "Leave the dead to bury their own dead; you must go and spread the news of the Kingdom of God."
Yet another man said to him, "Master, I am going to follow you, but let me first say goodbye to my people at home."
Jesus said to him, "No one who puts his hand to the plough, and then looks back, is fitted for the Kingdom of God."

At first glance, these words seem exceedingly harsh, but we must remember that Jesus was calling for workers who would go with him from place to place. He never failed to warn his would-be followers that they must count the cost. No unwilling conscripts could be used in the sacrificial endeavor upon which he was engaged.

Since his work brought Jesus into conflict with so many accepted patterns of life, allegiance to him often meant the severing of family ties. Indeed, it did for Jesus himself. The one picture of Jesus' contact with his own family that is preserved in the early tradition reveals their misunderstanding of his zeal. They sought to take him home to his carpenter shop, but Jesus answered, "Who are my mother and my brothers? . . . Whoever does the will of God is my brother and sister and mother" (Mark 3:33, 35). Jesus realized that a conflict between the generations was sometimes unavoidable. He had not come to bring peace, but division. "For I have come to turn a man against his father

38

and a daughter against her mother-in-law, and a man's enemies will be in his own household" (Matthew 10:35–36). Such cases were probably extreme, but they show how complete was the loyalty that Jesus demanded of those who were to follow him.

A prominent contact of Jesus was with *the sick*. Amidst the ignorance and filth of the ancient Orient, disease was inevitably widespread. Our tradition is unanimous in ascribing to Jesus a unique gift of healing. Wherever he found sickness, he sought to bring a healing touch that would awaken faith and new life. These events had a most important religious significance. Two theories of the cause of disease were held in ancient Palestine. According to one, sickness was a punishment for sin. There are cases where that is undoubtedly true, but it is just as certain that it is impossible to conclude from any particular sickness that the man has sinned. The other theory was that sickness was due to demon possession. That strikes us as an even less defensible theory. But we must remember that bacteria had not yet been discovered. In essence, the theory of demon possession meant that illness was caused by forces working against the will of God, and not by God himself. To heal disease, therefore, was to further the work of God. It is an entirely mistaken idea to suppose that Jesus sought to avoid a healing ministry. Rather, he pointed to these cures as the chief evidence that the rule of God was beginning to dawn. The demons were giving way before the spirit of God.

As an illustration of these healing contacts of Jesus, we shall use the first story that Mark offers. It will be noted that the evangelist pictures a conversation between Jesus and the foul spirit that was supposed to afflict the man (Mark 1:23–28):

There was in their synagogue a man under the control of a foul spirit, and he cried out,

"What do you want of us, Jesus, you Nazarene? Have you come to destroy us? I know who you are, you are God's holy One!"

Jesus reproved him, and said, "Silence! Get out of him!"

The foul spirit convulsed the man and gave a loud cry and went out of him. And they were all so amazed that they discussed it with one another, and said, "What does this mean? It is a new teaching! He gives orders with authority, even to the foul spirits, and they obey him!"

Great progress has been made through the centuries in medical science, but no one has surpassed Jesus in compassion for the sick. No one today can be concerned for the kingdom of God and minimize the alleviation of physical suffering.

Another group with whom Jesus had many contacts was *the notoriously sinful.* To understand the importance of this, we must appreciate the ideal of piety that was then officially approved. The Pharisees formed associations within which they made their purchases in order that they might be sure that they ate no untithed vegetables. Those who, from ignorance, indifference, or poverty, neglected the minute requirements of the law were "sinners" with whom they were to have no dealings. The tax collectors were among the most notorious. The attitude of Jesus seems to have been quite the opposite of Pharisaic isolationism. He had come to seek and to save the lost sheep of the house of Israel. A typical incident is reported in these words (Mark 2:15-17):

He was at table in his house, with many tax-collectors and irreligious people who were at table with him and his disciples, for there were many of them among his followers. And when the scribes who were of the Pharisees' party saw that he was eating with irreligious people and tax-collectors, they said to his disciples,

"Why does he eat with tax-collectors and irreligious people?"

Jesus heard it and said to them, "It is not well people but the sick who have to have the doctor. I did not come to invite the pious but the irreligious."

We have already noted the significance of this ministry for the message of Jesus. In defending his conduct at this point, Jesus appealed to the action of God. If he was seeking the lost, it was because that was the purpose of God. He had greater joy at the repentance of these irreligious people than with the religious conformity of the self-righteous. After they had friendly association with Jesus, the words "your sins are forgiven" (Luke 7:48) took on new meaning, for they came from the lips of one who incarnated reconciling love. It was this activity of Jesus that laid the foundation for the word in the gospel of John, "Whoever has seen me has seen the Father."

The contacts of Jesus with *non-Jews* are especially important for the theme of this study. It appears that he did not deliberately extend his ministry to those of other races and nations. According to the earlier tradition, he did not work among Samaritans, the half-Jews who lived between Galilee and Judea. Many Gentiles were to be found in Palestine, and it is clear that Jesus did not shut himself off entirely from them. One such meeting was described as follows (Matthew 8:5-10, 13):

A Roman captain came up and appealed to him, saying, "My servant, sir, is lying sick with paralysis at my house, in great distress."

He said to him, "I will come and cure him."

But the captain answered, "I am not a suitable person, sir, to have you come under my roof, but simply say the word, and my servant will be cured. For I am myself under the orders of others and I have soldiers under me, and I tell one to go, and he goes, and another to come, and he comes, and my slave to do something, and he does it."

When Jesus heard this he was astonished, and said to his followers, "I tell you, I have not found anyone in Israel with such faith as this."

Then Jesus said to the captain, "Go! You shall find it just as you believe!"

If Jesus found Gentiles so much more responsive than Jews, why did he not turn to them when his mission to his own people was proving unsuccessful? It is clear that he did not. When he was importuned by a Syrophoenician woman to heal her daughter, Jesus insisted that his work was first of all for his own people. According to that story, it was only because of the woman's clever rejoinder that he later consented to help. True, like the great prophets of old, Jesus envisaged a time in the future when Gentiles would enter the kingdom of God (Matthew 8:11-12) :

I tell you, many will come from the east and from the west and take their places at the feast with Abraham, Isaac and Jacob in the Kingdom of Heaven.

But that did not mean that Jesus felt any call to carry his own message beyond Israel.

The modern reader will not understand this apparent restriction and narrowness until he comes to appreciate the messianic framework of the ministry of Jesus. The Master did not look upon himself as simply a wise man teaching all men a satisfying way of life; his work was inseparably related to the kingdom of God. The preparation for its coming must be made among the people with whom God had stood in this special relation. This meant a concentration of effort, not with the thought of excluding other nations, but for their ultimate inclusion. Though his work was not *among* all peoples, it was still true that it was a work *for* all peoples.

One other group of Jesus' contacts must be considered, those with *his opponents*. Although he came to bring good news to men, inevitably Jesus stirred up intense enmity. This did not come primarily from the irreligious. As we have seen, many of these welcomed him with joy, as one who brought release from too difficult burdens. It was the pillars of society of whom Jesus ran afoul. The religious and political leaders did not repent, but turned against the popular Galilean prophet; and in a few short months, they brought his earthly career to an untimely close.

One group of opponents does not bulk large in our tradition. They were the "zealots" who desired a holy war of deliverance against Rome. Jesus quickly made it clear that his aims included no such political objective. Do twice the impressed service that is required, rather than imagine that the kingdom of God could be brought near by bloody revolution! It was first at Jerusalem that Jesus came into contact with the aristocratic party of Sadducees. We are not to suppose, however, that difference of opinion with them over the resurrection of the dead was a contributing cause to his own death. Jews looked upon such aspects of belief as a private matter; it was in their way of life that conformity was demanded.

The Pharisees were the real religious leaders of Palestine, and in many ways Jesus stood closer to them than to any other group. He and they were alike in their religious zeal, yet there were many points of conflict between them. We have already noted the difference in attitude toward the tax collectors and the irreligious. Many of their disputes concerned the keeping of the sabbath, for Jesus refused to be bound by the current proscriptions against work when human life was in need through sickness or hunger. "The Sabbath was made for man, not man for the Sabbath" (Mark 2:27). He criticized, too, their emphasis on externals and their meticulous regulations to avoid ritual defilement. "Nothing that goes into a man from outside can pollute him. It is what comes out of a man that pollutes him" (Mark 7:15).

Important as these differences were for the career of Jesus, it would be untrue to suppose that the Pharisees were responsible for his death. It was the political authorities who really brought about his end. It appears that Jesus had to avoid Galilee during the closing months of his life because of the murderous opposition of Herod, the tetrarch. The high priestly party at Jerusalem were as much the representatives of civil authority as of religious worship, so that when Jesus drove the money changers and sellers of sacrificial animals out of the temple they saw a threat to their power. Moreover, Pilate was certain to look upon one who proclaimed a kingdom other than the Roman as a dangerous individual. True, Jesus did not reject the payment of taxes to Rome, although if a man gave his whole soul and life to God, there was little left for the emperor. Neither did his work present an immediate political threat. But the authorities were taking no chances. Through the perfidy of one of the disciples, Jesus was quietly seized by the temple police after he had celebrated a last supper with the inner circle. The high priest and the council turned him over to Pilate for trial. It was probably on the morning of

44

April 7, 30 A.D. that Jesus was crucified as "King of the Jews," along with two thieves, at a place called Golgotha.

These bald facts are quickly recorded. Considered thus, the career of Jesus might not seem to have world-shaking significance. When he died, it is unlikely that his name was known outside Palestine. He had fewer followers than Father Divine or Aimee Semple McPherson has today. But this was not to be the end of his career; it was only the beginning. A faith had been kindled from his life that could not long be interred. Those who had thought that it was he who should redeem Israel were to find even greater things in store. Contact with Jesus was still to set the hearts of men and women aglow. If he no longer went with them in the flesh along the roads of Palestine, he was to lead them in the spirit to the ends of the earth.

CHAPTER VI

The Witness of the Early Church

THE EARLIEST CHRISTIAN MESSAGE was not confined to repeating the sayings of Jesus; nor did it consist simply in the recital of anecdotes from his life. Peter, James, John, and Paul proclaimed the revolutionary significance that they had found in him. From the very beginning, Christianity was a faith about Jesus. Believers were certain that he was God's deliverer and that his coming was the focal point of all human history. The old world was passing away; in him, all things would be created anew.

The central conviction was that God had raised from the dead this Jesus who had been "crucified under Pontius Pilate." This was variously conceived in the New Testament, and we must take care not to be led aside into the discussion of problems which are not central to that faith. The truth that mattered was not that Jesus had associated with his disciples for a short time after his death. That would have been a very satisfying experience to these friends, but it could never have become the basis for a new religion. The essential thing was that God had vindicated his anointed one by raising him from the dead. The verdict of Pilate had been set aside by the ultimate judge of all men. The new age, which was to be introduced by the resurrection of the dead, had in principle already begun, for God had raised

Jesus from the dead and exalted him to the right hand of power.

The proof for this was found in appearances of the risen Christ to chosen witnesses. It was not inability to discover a dead body that produced the Christian message. It was that they had found a risen Christ. The earliest account we possess is that from Paul, in his letter to the church at Corinth. Since he reported it as the faith that he himself had received, and he was the earliest Christian writer, this is as far back as we can go (I Corinthians 15:3-8):

For I passed on to you, as of first importance, the account I had received, that Christ died for our sins, as the Scriptures foretold, that he was buried, that on the third day he was raised from the dead, as the Scriptures foretold, and that he was seen by Cephas, and then by the Twelve. After that he was seen by more than five hundred brothers at one time, most of whom are still alive, although some of them have fallen asleep. Then he was seen by James, then by all the apostles, and finally he was seen by me also, as though I were born at the wrong time.

Through this concise statement, the key developments of the early Church may be traced. The reasons for the leadership of Cephas (Peter), James, and Paul are to be found in the experiences recounted here.

Instead of dealing with a generalized picture of the message of the early Church, we shall examine three sermons that have been preserved from various outstanding leaders. Certain differences between them will be found, but all agree in the central conviction—namely that God had performed a unique act for man's deliverance in the coming of Jesus, the Christ. The message did not deal with good advice as to how men should live, nor with techniques by which they might discover God. It dealt with how *God had sought them* through a decisive event in history. They believed that they were proclaiming the word and deed of God.

For the first of our sermons, we shall examine the words ascribed to Peter as having been delivered fifty days after the crucifixion. Although the sermon is pointed for this particular occasion, its importance for us lies in the fact that it represents the type of message often delivered by many early Christians. The point of departure was the ecstatic behavior of the followers of Jesus, which some visitors at Pentecost interpreted as intoxication. Peter assured them that it was due to the outpouring of the spirit of God, which had been expected before the coming of his kingdom. Then he continued (Acts 2:22-24, 32-33):

Men of Israel . . . Jesus of Nazareth, as you know, was a man whom God commended to you by the wonders, portents, and signs that God did right among you through him. But you, by the fixed purpose and intention of God, handed him over to wicked men, and had him crucified. But God set aside the pain of death and raised him up. [There follows a long proof of this from Scripture].
. . . and to his resurrection we are all witnesses. So he has been exalted to God's right hand, and has received from his Father and poured over us the holy Spirit that had been promised.

Luke asserts that this was spoken to men who had gathered from all parts of the world. Naturally, it is only a very brief summary of what Peter and the others said. Many of the stories preserved in our gospels must have been used to amplify these bald assertions. But the message came to a focus in the cross and the resurrection. It is significant to note what is left out. We find no teaching about the nature

48

of God. That was of course assumed, but the new thing was not an entirely novel *idea* of God; a new *act* had been performed by the God, whom they had known all along. Likewise, the sermon contains nothing in the way of moral teaching. It was not because this was unimportant, but the first word of Peter was not about higher ideals of conduct since his hearers already knew higher ethical standards than they were able to live up to. Rather, he called upon them to repent and receive forgiveness, in view of the fact that God had vindicated the one whom they had handed over to death.

The proclamation that Jesus was the Messiah has, I fear, little meaning to a modern student. He expects no such functionary, any more than did the Greeks to whom the message was later taken. They called Jesus Savior and Lord and other terms from their own background of experience, which might indicate the fact that he had brought them deliverance and was recognized as their rightful leader. If Peter's sermon does not include all that we would say today, it is instructive that it did not satisfy completely the later apostolic preachers. New situations led to a deeper understanding of the message. As it was taken from the Aramaic language, in which Peter had spoken in Jerusalem, to a Greek-speaking and Greek-thinking world, transformations were inevitable. It had to be made intelligible to men and women of very different background, who were living, not in Jewish ghettos, but in the cultural milieu of the Roman Empire. It is striking, however, that despite the changed circumstances, the theme remained essentially the same.

For our second sermon, we shall turn to the Apostle Paul. At the height of his powers, Paul wrote a letter to the church at Rome to prepare the way for his coming to the capital city. It gives the most systematic presentation of his conception of the Christian faith, particularly in its relation to the Judaism that he no longer accepted. Undoubtedly he had hammered out these sentences through years of public preaching on these themes. He attempts to give a logical statement of why he could now say, "For me to live is Christ" (Philippians 1:21). Selections from two of the central paragraphs will be quoted (Romans 3:20-25 and 5:1-2, 6-8, 10):

For no human being can be made upright in the sight of God by observing the Law. All that the Law can do is to make men conscious of sin. But now God's way of uprightness has been disclosed without any reference to law, though the Law and the Prophets bear witness to it. It is God's way of uprightness and comes through having faith in Jesus Christ, and it is for all who have faith, without distinction. For all men sin and come short of the glory of God, but by his mercy they are made upright for nothing, by the deliverance secured through Christ Jesus. For God showed him publicly dying as a sacrifice of reconciliation to be taken advantage of through faith.

So as we have been made upright by faith, let us live in peace with God through our Lord Jesus Christ, by whom we have been introduced through faith to the favor of God that we now enjoy. . . . For when we were still helpless, at the decisive moment Christ died for us godless men. Why, a man will hardly give his life for an upright person, though perhaps for a really good man some may be brave enough to die. But God proves his love for us by the fact that Christ died for us when we were still sinners. . . . If when we were God's enemies, we were reconciled to him through the death of his Son, it is far more certain that now that we are reconciled we shall be saved through sharing in his life.

What was Paul trying to say through the terminology and

concepts of his time? He was asserting that a satisfactory life could never be attained simply by man's own efforts. Man can never fulfil the expectation of God, but lives in enmity toward him. Paul had just shown that this was true of Jew and Gentile alike. There was no way to reconciliation with God from the side of man. But God himself had taken the initiative. It was not through any merit of man, but because we were sinners. God had shown his love by the fact that Christ had died for us. In the background of Paul's mind was the procedure of the law courts. Man had been acquitted, not on the basis of what he could pay, but through what God had freely done for him in the death and resurrection of Christ. Man had only to receive this by faith. And that is what Paul meant by "faith": receiving what God had done for him in Christ, restoring to fellowship with him. "God through Christ reconciled the world to himself" (II Corinthians 5:19).

It is impossible for us, in this brief examination, to see all that this meant in the full perspective of Paul's world view, a world in which there were many obstacles separating man and God. The essential thing is that Paul found all these removed in Christ. In him was a full and sufficient revelation of redemptive love. Jesus was not simply the highest of men who had suffered a noble martyr's death; he was the one through whom all that was involved in God's salvation had come to men. So Paul bursts out (II Corinthians 9:15 and Romans 8:38–39):

Thank God for his indescribable gift. . . . I am convinced that neither death nor life nor angels nor their hierarchies nor the present nor the future nor any supernatural forces either of height or depth will be able to separate us from the love God has shown in Christ Jesus our Lord.

51

Our last sermon comes, according to early tradition, from John. It does not give a messianic interpretation of the career of Jesus; nor is it couched in terms of the difficult arguments of Paul. It is a simple and yet profound assertion of the love that is at the heart of Christian faith (I John 4:7-11):

Dear friends, let us love one another, for love comes from God, and everyone who loves is a child of God and knows God. Whoever does not love does not know God, for God is love. God's love for us has been revealed in this way—that God has sent his only Son into the world, let us have life through him. The love consists not in our having loved God, but in his loving us and sending his Son as an atoning sacrifice for our sins. Dear friends, if God has loved us so, we ought to love one another.

Nowhere has the nature of Christian love been set forth more clearly. It is not, first of all, a love that man has for God. The mystic's quest for union with the perfect reality is not what John and the other early Christians meant by "love." Love had had its source in God's act for men in sending his son. "God loved the world so much that he gave his only Son, so that no one who believes in him should be lost, but that they should all have eternal life" (John 3:16). Man's love should be a response to that love. Here lay the supreme motivation for our love. It is our grateful response to what God has done for us in Christ. It is useless to talk about knowing God if our lives do not show this evidence of being transformed by him. The only way in which a man can show his gratitude for God's love lies in revealing the same spirit toward others.

Here the Christian faith is reduced to its simplest possible terms. We need to fill in these interpretations with all possible knowledge of the Jesus who is evaluated in this way. We are called upon to experiment and study in order to see how we may show love effectively to our fellow men. The New Testament is not a rule book where all the answers to life's duties are written down. It is the inspiring record of the revelation of God's love that should provide the stimulation for self-giving devotion to the needs of men. So the Jesus of the Gospel of John says, "Just as I have loved you, you must love one another. By this they will all know that you are my disciples—by your love for one another" (John 13:35).

As we look back over these statements of the Christian message, several common characteristics stand out:

1. Jesus Christ is at its very heart and center; the gospel is an interpretation of his significance.

2. Yet the gospel is not simply a message about a historical character, but about God's activity through him.

3. The message is primarily a testimony; some argument is to be found, but it is first of all a witness.

4. The message deals, not with cosmological speculation, but with the activity of God in history. It does not set forth a theory of the universe, but how man may come into fellowship with the determiner of destiny.

5. God is not the impersonal object of man's search, but one who "in these latter days has spoken to us in a Son" (Hebrews 1:2).

When the gospel was translated into terms of Greek thought, much of this was changed. Whether that was fortunate is a matter of difference of opinion. Man had to think about the message and relate it to the rest of his world view, and the Greek philosophy of the time provided the framework. Inevitably, there is the same need in our day. But a crucial question faces us at this point: Will the essential nature of the gospel be retained, or will it be transformed into something else? Are we dealing in the New Testament simply with obsolete religious ideas of the ancient world, or do we face a supreme revelation of God?

That is a question that can only be answered by a decision of faith. Naturally, there is nothing else by which the gospel can be proved. If there were, that would be more ultimate than the truth which is claimed to be final. There is no appeal except to the whole of life experience. It is instructive that the New Testament writers do not argue *for* the good news; they argue *from* it. They sought to work out its implications in life. The words of the gospel of John are still true. "Anyone who resolves to do his will will know whether my teaching comes from God, or originates with me" (John 7:17).

CHAPTER VII

A Universal Gospel

CHRISTIANITY began as a Jewish sect which proclaimed that the name of God's Messiah was Jesus. But within a few years, it became a new religion that embraced all peoples. The winning of a truly universal gospel made it possible for the message to be carried to us. Here was the crucial choice that the apostles faced: Should they remain within the fold of Jewish nationalism, or was Jesus to be proclaimed as the Lord to whom *every* knee should bow?

The issue probably arose gradually. Quite early, the gospel was preached to Samaritans; and doubtless individual Gentiles in Palestine were baptized into the name of Jesus. But we must remember that proselytes were continually being received by Jews themselves, and we are not told on what basis these Christian converts were received. According to the Acts of the Apostles, it was at Antioch, the metropolis of the Near East, that Greeks first came into the Church in considerable numbers. Soon after this, two missionaries from that church, Barnabas and Paul, founded some communities in southern Asia Minor. The main body of the Jews rejected their message, but the Gentiles received it gladly.

The decision could not be postponed any longer. It was no longer a question of a few exceptional cases; the principle had to be decided. When a Gentile was baptized into the name of the Lord Jesus, did that place him under the obligation of receiving circumcision and obeying the Jewish law? If that demand seems ridiculous to modern American Christians it only serves to emphasize the long road that has been traveled. In 46 A.D., this expectation seemed self-evident to many devoted men. They rejoiced in the fact that many Gentiles were turning to the Lord, but they assumed that the law was to be obeyed by all. Were not the promises in scripture for the children of Abraham? Was not the covenant that God had made with Abraham one that had been sealed with the rite of circumcision? Had not Jesus himself said, "As long as heaven and earth endure, not one dotting of an *i* or crossing of a *t* will be dropped from the Law until it is all observed" (Matthew 5:18)?

One version of the controversy is recorded in Acts 15. It portrays James, the brother of Jesus, as the ultimate authority. It makes clear that the demand for the circumcision of Gentile believers was rejected after the inspiring testimony of the missionaries had been heard. A more vivid account comes from one of the disputants. Some years later, when Paul faced a continuation of the same crisis in some of his churches, he wrote to the Galatians (Galatians 2:15):

I went up to Jerusalem again, with Barnabas, and took Titus also with me. It was in obedience to a revelation that I went. I laid before them the good news that I preach to the heathen, presenting it privately to the leaders, for fear my efforts might be or might have been futile. But they did not insist that even my companion Titus, although he was a Greek, should be circumcised, to gratify the false brothers who had been smuggled in, who sneaked in to spy upon the freedom we enjoy in Christ Jesus so as to reduce us to slavery again. But we did not submit to them for a moment, in order that the truth of the good news might remain yours.

The realism of Paul in this incident should be noted. His opponents were ready with an abundance of arguments, based on scripture, which were to prove up to the hilt that obedience to the law was essential for salvation. Paul met them with the testimony of life and fact. Here was Titus, an uncircumcised Greek. What was there lacking in his religious experience? What grace of the spirit did he fail to possess? If the love of God through Christ, working in the heart of Titus, could achieve this, what man was to say that the other Gentiles had to enter the kingdom of God through the door of the Jewish law? It is unfortunate that some of the later debates in the Christian Church over what is essential have not been resolved by the same kind of realism. It is still true as in the day of Paul, "What is written kills, but the Spirit gives life" (II Corinthians 3:6).

The importance of the decision taken at Jerusalem cannot be too much emphasized. If it had gone the other way, the sect of the Nazarenes (as the Jewish Christians were called by the Pharisees) would undoubtedly have been reabsorbed into national Judaism. The settlement had implications that are of permanent significance. The peculiar customs of one people (even when supported by long religious sanction) cannot be made an essential part of the Christian faith. Religious rites that may be very precious to some cannot be made obligatory upon all. "Means of grace," which some find helpful, are not to be included among the "essentials of faith." New forms of this problem have arisen from time to time, but the principle was decided when Paul won the fight for Gentile freedom at Jerusalem years ago.

Further complications were soon to arise. As so often happens, the solving of one difficulty only opened up another. Although obedience to the Old Testament law was not required from Gentiles as a part of their religious discipline, it was assumed that Jewish Christians would continue to observe its demands. To the end of his life, the Jewish festivals and customs were precious to Paul. Why should a Jew or any other national give up traditional customs of his people so long as they are morally neutral and he does not look upon them as an essential demand for salvation? But paramount among these were the food laws. Jews did not eat with Gentiles, for they had to be sure that everything met *kosher* regulations. The central Christian act of worship, however, was a community meal, the celebration of the Lord's Supper. If Gentiles were not required to obey the law, how could Jews continue to eat with them at the same Lord's Table? Paul describes for us how that issue arose at Antioch (Galatians 2:11-14):

When Cephas came to Antioch, I opposed him to his face, for his own conduct condemned him. For until some people came from James, he used to eat with the heathen, but after they came, he began to draw back and hold aloof, for fear of the party of circumcision. The other Jewish Christians followed his example in concealing their real views, so that even Barnabas was carried away by their pose.

Paul may have been somewhat ungenerous in accusing those who disagreed with him of hypocritical conduct. We must see, however, that the issue was no longer that of *sending* the gospel to those of other races; it was the question of *living* with them on the basis of real brotherhood. There are plenty of illustrations today of good and sincere people (within their insight) who would contribute liberally to send Christian missionaries to other races but who would not sit down at a meal with those people in Christian

58

brotherhood. But here at Antioch, it was not merely a matter of social intercourse; the meal in question included the celebration of the Lord's Supper. Therefore, the issue involved a division in Christian worship. It meant that two groups who served the same Master could not join in a common memorial and in heavenly feeding from their Lord.

Paul became so excited in telling the Galatians how he criticized Cephas that he failed to state how the difficulty at Antioch was resolved. It is entirely possible that Paul was defeated on that issue and that, for a time, a compromise was reached in Palestine and Syria to enable the Gentiles to eat with the Jews without offending the customs of the latter. But Paul won out in the end, because the churches that he founded in Europe were essentially Gentile churches. There the standard of complete brotherhood was maintained. The principle was established that distinctions of race and nationality could no longer divide those who looked to Christ in faith (Galatians 3:26–28):

For in Christ Jesus you are all sons of God through your faith. For all of you who have been baptized into union with Christ have clothed yourselves with Christ. There is no room for "Jew" and "Greek"; there is no room for "slave" and "freemen"; there is no room for "male" and "female," for in union with Christ Jesus you are all one.

Such questions as circumcision and Jewish food laws have little interest for young people today. But even the most provincial realize how crucial is the issue whether the Christion Church can transcend the divisions of race and nationality and bind men and women together into an indivisible brotherhood. Although the specific aspects of the problem have changed, the underlying issue is the same. We would do well to have the patience to learn how Paul defended his universal gospel when narrow nationalists tried to upset the faith of the Galatian churches. To this day, his letter to them is the most important charter of Christian liberty. In a world that is struggling to attain various freedoms, we should examine the liberty that Paul ascribes to Christ.

First of all, it should be noted that nowhere does Paul appeal either to the example or the teaching of Jesus to establish his position. On other subjects he occasionally did so, but here the situation was different. We have seen in an earlier chapter that Jesus had carried on no mission among non-Jews. While he had taken a free attitude on table intercourse, he had not repudiated the law. We do not know whether Paul's opponents appealed to the traditions about Jesus, but Paul insisted that he was not dependent on the original apostles for his understanding of the faith. It had come to him "by revelation." Some of us believe that this included hard thinking on the implications of the death and resurrection of Christ, but let Paul use his own vocabulary. The fact remains that he did not solve this problem by appeal to either the teaching or example of Jesus. He thought it through in terms of the whole meaning of the coming of Christ. This has far-reaching implications for us. If less than twenty years after the crucifixion the greatest problem that faced the early Church could not be solved by an appeal to any word of Jesus, it is unreasonable to expect that nineteen hundred years later Christians should solve their problems by an appeal to the recorded words of Jesus.

Paul did not deny that the promises of God were made to the children of Abraham. In other words, he did not attempt to cut Christianity off from its Jewish roots. No one knew better than he that it was to this people that the great essentials of monotheistic faith had been revealed.

Paul agreed with his opponents that only the children of Abraham might be saved. But how did people become children of Abraham? It was not through a fleshly operation, but through having faith in God like Abraham's. Paul appealed to a spiritual heredity. Men were not saved by faith *and* some legally prescribed ritual; it was by faith, and faith only.

But since the law came *after* the time of Abraham, did it not represent a legitimate development of the demand of God? Is not the later an advance on the earlier? On the contrary, Paul did not believe that the requirements of God had changed. Although certain objectives were attained through the law during the time of its sway, that period was now over. The death of Christ had closed accounts with the law, and men were now freed from its dominion. Paul worked this out by a subtle *ad hominem* argument that is much less important to us than is his major conviction, which is valid even though some of his reasoning may not strike the modern student as too conclusive. God has delivered men from the tyranny of finding salvation through the meticulous observance of hundreds of commands. Man has been set free by a great revelation of divine love that leaves him no longer in the status of a slave, but as a son in the household of God.

Freedom is the indispensable prerequisite for moral conduct, but in itself it is negative. Liberty does not lighten the world. By their misuse of freedom, millions seek to put out the lights by which men see. The removal of outward restraints is always dangerous unless they are replaced by inward checks. Civilized man cannot live in complete independence of his fellows, and his freedom must always be limited by the rights of others. True freedom is not irresponsibility. Freedom is the ability to express your noblest self with inner sincerity. Paul believed that Christ had made that possible (Galatians 5:1, 13-14):

This is the freedom with which Christ has freed us. So stand firm in it, and do not get under a yoke of slavery again.

. . . Only do not make your freedom an excuse for the physical, but in love be slaves to one another. For the whole law is summed up in one saying: "You must love your neighbor as you do yourself."

Paul had seen many who thought that freedom meant doing as you please. Starting out with this goal, they ended by becoming slaves to their own appetites. Freedom from the law did not mean liberty to indulge their physical cravings; it meant a freedom to be guided by the spirit of God, "What the Spirit produces is love, joy, peace, patience, kindness, goodness, faithfulness, gentleness, self-control. There is no law against such things" (Galatians 5:22-23). And Paul might well have added, "No law can ever produce them." Laws may restrain misconduct, but they can never lead men into adventurous avenues of good will. That comes from a freedom which is controlled from within by a high and noble purpose; it comes through one who is liberated from conflicting desires so that he can channel his energies to a worthy end. This is the liberty that Paul said was possible through Christ.

CHAPTER VIII

The World Outlook of the New Testament

From BEGINNING TO END, our New Testament has a world outlook. Although there was a time, at the beginning of the movement initiated by Jesus, when the full implications were not yet realized, all of the books of our New Testament were written by men who took it for granted that Christian faith was for all men. Those who did not transcend national particularism were soon left by the wayside. In this final chapter, we shall survey the chief writings of the New Testament to see how their authors expressed this breadth of view.

The Gospel of Matthew contains the most narrow and particularistic expressions in the New Testament. Some of its traditions clearly come from Jewish Christians who had not yet been emancipated from religious nationalism. But the framework reveals an author with a wider vision. He began his account of the "King of the Jews" with the story of "wise men" who came from the East to bring their treasures and to pay their homage. This reflects the world-wide significance that was claimed for Jesus. His coming concerned all peoples. For the conclusion of his gospel, Matthew pictured the risen Christ coming to the mountain in

Galilee to which he had directed his disciples. To them, he gave this command and this promise (Matthew 28:18–20):

Full authority in heaven and on earth has been given to me. Therefore go and make disciples of all the heathen, baptize them in the name of the Father, the Son, the holy Spirit, and teach them to observe all the commands that I have given you. I will always be with you, to the very close of the age.

Naturally, this saying has held a very prominent place in the history of the later Christian missions. It is the charter for the belief that although the ministry of the earthly Jesus was to his own people, his ultimate purpose, as revealed through his risen presence, included the saving of all the children of men. Those who were obedient to that call would find his continuing presence with them. This conviction has been amply corroborated in the experience of the Church through the ages.

Luke and the Acts of the Apostles must be considered together, for they comprise a single, two-volume work. The author was certainly a Gentile and eager at every point to emphasize the world-wide scope of the gospel. He did not trace the genealogy of Jesus back to Abraham, the father of the Jews; he extended the family tree back to Adam, the father of the whole human race. Although he did not, as Paul did, call Jesus the "second Adam," yet in this way he emphasized that all of humanity is involved in the work of Jesus. The theme for his volumes is this: "The message that was first offered to the Jews has been rejected by them, and hence it has been carried to the Gentiles." In order to introduce that theme at once, Luke transferred the story of the rejection at Nazareth to the opening of his account of Jesus' ministry. The announcement that the messianic time had come was met by his hearers with astonishment and incredulity. The prophet was not honored in his own country. The evangelist went on, then, to show that even in Old Testament times the favor of God was not confined to Jews (Luke 4:25-27):

There were plenty of widows in Israel in Elijah's time, when the sky was closed for three years and a half, and Elijah was not sent to one of them, but to a widow at Zarephath in Sidon. And there were plenty of lepers in Israel in the time of the prophet Elisha, and none of them was cured, but Naaman, the Syrian.

Matthew and Mark had told of a preaching journey of the twelve disciples. Their number was symbolical of the restoration of the twelve tribes of Israel. But Luke added also the sending of seventy (or seventy-two) others and located this during a trip, which he described, through Samaria, non-Jewish territory. According to popular belief, this was the number of the nations of the world. Clearly, the evangelist meant to suggest by the sending out of the seventy (or seventy-two) that the message of Jesus was for all peoples. A little later, he gave his version of the great supper, which, as we have seen, was spoken by Jesus to defend his mission to the religious outcasts of Israel. But Luke added a further touch in his version. After the poor, the maimed, the blind, and the lame have come in from the streets of the city, the slave said (Luke 14:22-23):

"What you ordered, sir, has been done, and there is still room." And the master said to the slave, "Go out on the roads, and among the hedges, and make them come in, so that my house may be full."

Luke was thinking here of the Gentiles, for whom there was place at the banquet of God since those first invited had refused to come.

In his second volume, Luke set the keynote, as Matthew had done, through a word of the risen Lord. "You will be witnesses for me in Jerusalem, and all over Judea and Samaria and to the very ends of the earth" (Acts 1:8). He pictured the first testimony on the day of Pentecost, when a great crowd from all over the earth had gathered in Jerusalem (Acts 2:9-11):

. . . Parthians, Medes, Elamites, residents of Mesopotamia, of Judea and Cappadocia, of Pontus and Asia, of Phrygia and Pamphylia, of Egypt and the district of Africa about Cyrene, visitors from Rome, Jews and proselytes, Cretans and Arabs. . . .

What a vivid description of the peoples about the Mediterannean and to the East! We are not told, however, whether any of these carried the message back to their homelands. Likewise, the apostles appear to be strangely stationary for men who had just received a world-wide commission. As a matter of fact, it was the rough hand of persecution that first thrust them out of Jerusalem. But God has used stranger ways than this to forward his work.

In a very skilful way, Luke portrays the widening horizon of Christian propaganda. First it is carried to the Samaritans. Then we read of the baptism of a eunuch, according to Jewish law ineligible for admission to Judaism. Then Peter has a part in the conversion of Cornelius, a Roman centurion, together with his whole household. Finally, at Antioch, the gospel is definitely preached to Greeks; and out from the Greek church go missionaries to the wider world to experience, in city after city, its rejection by the Jews and its acceptance by the Gentiles. Luke's story may be more schematic than actual history. Naturally, his information concerning the earliest days was limited; but his theme was deeply grounded in the facts of development.

Christianity had emerged through these stages as a world faith.

We must suppose that many zealous missionaries were busy in propagating the faith. The only one, however, about whom adequate information has been preserved is Paul, who stood out as Luke's hero. Luke tells how Paul, after planting the gospel in southern Asia Minor, moved over to Europe. The Macedonian cities of Philippi, Thessalonica, and Berea were evangelized. After an unfortunate failure in Athens, he founded a strong church in Corinth, from which the message spread throughout Achaia. Then, moving over to Ephesus, he made that city his headquarters for a campaign in the province of Asia. When his work was complete, Paul revisited his Macedonian and Achaian churches and undertook a final trip to Jerusalem before passing through Rome to Spain, where he intended to embark on new missionary labors. But his arrest in the temple at Jerusalem cut short these endeavors, and the book ends with the arrival of Paul in Rome as a prisoner.

It has taken but a few sentences to sketch this outline of Paul's gigantic labors. But the modern reader must remember that Paul did most of that traveling on foot. In the face of incredible hardships and difficulties, he hurried on to make his Lord known to more and more men. He labored amid persecution and bitter attack, yet never losing his serene confidence in Christ and his unconquerable joy. It is no wonder that every herald of the cross of Christ has found in his intrepid zeal an inspiration second only to the Master himself. By writing his story, supplementing for us the letters of Paul, Luke made a tremendous contribution to the carrying of the gospel to lands unknown to these first-century missionaries.

It is recognized today that the Gospel of John is primarily

an interpretation of the Christian message as it appeared to this remarkable evangelist. Throughout the book, he assumes the bitter hostility of the Jews. In the prologue, it is stated of the Christ: "He came to his home, and his own family did not welcome him" (John 1:11). It is likewise assumed that the coming of Jesus is for all men. John the Baptist greets Jesus with the words: "There is God's lamb, who is to remove the world's sin!" (John 1:29). After a conversation with a Samaritan woman, Jesus is acclaimed by the most universal title in the New Testament; the Samaritans say of him: "We know that he is really the Savior of the world" (John 4:42). We read that before the close of his ministry, Greeks came seeking Jesus. When earlier the Jews suggest in scorn that Jesus intends to go away to teach the Greeks, the evangelist wanted to imply that this was exactly what had taken place; the risen Christ had gone to teach the Greeks.

The old charge that Jesus was "King of the Jews" is retained, but here Jesus tells Pilate that he is no earthly king. He is the king of truth; and he has come, not simply to fulfil Jewish hopes, but to witness to the truth (John 19:36–38). He is the Good Shepherd who has sheep of more than one fold (John 10:16). When this evangelist wrote, they were to be found among many peoples. The Jesus of the fourth gospel prays that they all may be *one,* as he and the Father are one (John 17:21). In this gospel, much of the older terminology has been sloughed off, and Jesus is seen in those universal features that have made it down the centuries the most popular of all with non-Jewish readers.

The universalism of Paul has been sufficiently shown through his sermons and letters, and through the story of his life as given by Luke. But there is one letter that bears his name, addressed to the Ephesians, which calls for special attention because it is especially directed to the problem of breaking down the barriers between peoples. The theme of the letter is *unity*; God has created one new man by breaking down the middle wall of partition separating Jew and Gentile. The most important passage should be quoted at length (Ephesians 2:11-19):

So remember that you were once physically heathen, and called uncircumcised by those who called themselves circumcised, though only physically, by human hands. At that time you had no connection with Christ, you were aliens to the commonwealth of Israel, and strangers to the agreements about God's promises; with no hope and no God in all the world. But now through your union with Christ you who were once far away have through the blood of Christ been brought near. For he is himself our peace. He has united the two divisions, and broken down the barrier that kept us apart, and through his human nature put an end to the feud between us, and abolished the Law with its rules and regulations, in order to make peace and create out of the two parties one new man by uniting them with himself, and to kill the feud between them with his cross and in one body reconcile them both to God with it. He came with the good news of peace for you who were far away and for those who were near; for it is through him that we both with one Spirit are now able to approach the Father. So you are no longer foreigners or strangers, but you are fellow-citizens of God's people and members of his family.

This remarkable passage testifies to the unity of humanity under God that the Christian message had been able to create. The barriers of prejudice and separation had been broken down through the realization that the work of Christ was for all. The bringing of peace with God had meant peace with one another. There could no longer be any thought of foreigners in the family of God. There could be no such thing as *foreign* missions, for God could not be a foreigner to any people. This author found the mystery of Christ in the fact that "through union with Christ Jesus the heathen are fellow heirs with the Jews, belong to the same body and share the promise with them" (Ephesians 3:6).

At first glance, the Letter to the Hebrews seems to be entirely within the Jewish world of thought. Its imagery is drawn from the Old Testament sacrificial worship; the heroes of faith that it portrays are exclusively Jewish; the comparisons of Jesus with other spiritual leaders are confined to the Hebrew horizon. Yet this superficial impression is entirely changed by closer examination. Jesus is presented as a priest of an entirely new type. The author received his suggestion from a Psalm word alluding to the old story incorporated in Genesis 14, where Abraham had paid tithes to Melchizedek, a priest-king whose name meant "king of righteousness." This king was not a Jew at all; yet the father of the "chosen people" had given him the highest token of respect. Jesus, insists the author of the letter, was a priest of this order. His priesthood did not depend on correct physical descent but, like Melchizedek, on his own inherent worth. Not through any Jewish rites prescribed in the Old Testament, but through the ministration of this Jesus had men secured perfect access to God.

All of the elaborate arguments based on the Jewish liturgy had one objective. This was to show that, for Christians, the Jewish law had been completely abolished. The coming of the new priesthood exercised by Jesus meant the invalidation of the levitic priesthood prescribed in the Penta-

70

teuch. Thus, in his own way, this author argued for the transcending of national particularism. The old in religion had been shaken to make way for the new (Hebrews 12:27-28):

Now the words . . . indicate the final removal of all that is shaken, as only created, leaving only what is unshaken to be permanent. Let us, therefore, be thankful that the kingdom given to us cannot be shaken, and so please God by worshiping him with reverence and awe. . . .

The last book in our New Testament bears the title of "Revelation." Its imagery is so strange to the modern reader that, to many, it is a book closed with seven seals. We can only note here, by way of general interpretation, that it was written to a group of churches in Asia Minor facing heavy persecution and expecting widespread martyrdoms because of the demand upon them to participate in the imperial worship. Here the cleavage is no longer between Jew and Gentile; it is between the Church and the world. The worshipers of the Beast, who symbolizes heathen power, stand opposed to the followers of the Lamb, the symbol for Christ. It is amazing how, throughout his book, the author assumes the world-wide spread of the Church and its universal character.

First, we may note his insistence that the judgments of God are over all (Revelation 14:6-7):

Then I saw another angel flying in mid-air with eternal good news to announce to the inhabitants of the earth, to every nation, tribe, language, and people. He cried in a loud voice, "Fear God and give him glory, for the hour of his judgment has come. Worship him who made heaven and earth and sea and the springs of water."

Second, we should note that the people whom Christ has

redeemed are drawn from "every tribe, tongue, people and nation, and he has made them a kingdom of priests for our God, and they are to reign over the earth" (Revelation 5:9–10). John sees in his vision that many will be martyred, and thus go to the presence of God (Revelation 7:9):

After that I saw a great crowd which no one could count from every nation, tribe, people, and language, standing before the throne and before the Lamb, wearing white robes, with palms in their hands.

But the seer was certain that the Beast would not finally be victorious over the followers of the Lamb. The triumph of God was sure. From the standpoint of eternity, it had already taken place (Revelation 11:15):

Then the seventh angel blew his trumpet, and loud voices were heard in heaven, saying, "The sovereignty of the world has passed into the possession of our Lord and his Christ, and he will reign forever and ever."

No more fitting conclusion could be found for our brief story of the world horizon of Christian faith. That Hallelujah Chorus rings from the throats of the Christian world at every Christmas season. But they are words of anticipation that wait fulfilment through the willing feet and loyal hearts of those who will make him known by word and deed and life. His reign has not yet come, and infinite misery still covers much of the earth. We do not yet see all things subject to him, but we see Jesus and would follow in his train.

72